ANIMAL TRACKERS
AROUND THE WORLD

ON SAFARI

Tessa Paul

CRABTREE
Publishing Company

CRABTREE
Publishing Company

350 Fifth Avenue
Suite 3308
New York, NY 10118

360 York Road, R.R.4
Niagara-on the-Lake
Ontario LOS IJO

73 Lime Walk
Headington, Oxford
England OX3 7AD

Editor **Greg Nickles**
Designer **Janelle Barker**
Consultant **Karen Jane Kemmis-Betty (M.Sc.)**

Illustrations
Andrew Beckett (cover background, track marks)
All other illustrations courtesy of Marshall Cavendish Partworks: Evi Antoniou (page 25); Robin Boutell/WLAA
(pages 4-5, 16-17); Wendy Bramell/WLAA (pages 4-5, 23); Robin Budden/WLAA (pages 10-11);
John Cox/WLAA (pages 4-5, 12, 14-15, 24-25); Matthew Hillier/WLAA (pages 6-7, 9); Alan Male/Linden Artists
(pages 6, 8); John Morris/WLAA (pages 13, 20-21); Steve Roberts/WLAA (page 22); Peter David Scott/WLAA
(page 26); Lindsay Seers (page 27); Kevin Toy (page 28); Simon Turvey/WLAA (pages 4-5, 18-19, 22);
Dan Wright (page 14)

First printed 1998
Copyright © 1998 Crabtree Publishing Company

Cataloging-in-Publication Data

Paul, Tessa

On safari / Tessa Paul
p. cm — (Animal trackers)
Includes index.
ISBN 0-86505 589-0 (library bound)   ISBN 0-86505-597-1 (pbk.)
Summary: Introduces the physical characteristics, behavior, and tracks of such
African animals as the elephant, giraffe, and crocodile.
1. Mammals—Africa—Juvenile literature. [1. Animals—Africa. 2. Animal tracks.]
I. Title. II. Series: Paul, Tessa. Animal trackers.
QL706.2.P425 1998   j599'.096   LC 98-10862
CIP

CONTENTS

ON SAFARI   4

ELEPHANT   6

ZEBRA   10

MEERKAT   12

RHINOCEROS   14

SPRINGBOK   16

GIRAFFE   18

LION   20

GALAGO   22

HIPPOPOTAMUS   24

LEOPARD   26

CROCODILE   30

INDEX   32

GLOSSARY   32

ON SAFARI

To go "on safari" is to trek across the African bush, following herds of giraffes, springboks, zebras, and elephants. On your way, you might spot a pride of lions, a toothy crocodile, or a tiny meerkat.

This book tells you how these animals live. It describes how some have patterned fur to help them blend into their surroundings. It tells you why the animals call to each other. When you are on safari, you will hear barks, roars, and wails. The calls may be a mating cry or a warning of danger!

The savannah is covered with tracks. These show the routes animals take as they search for food. Some of the animals eat only plants. Others eat meat. This book explains how both hunters and hunted live side by side. You will learn how springboks pronk to escape their enemies, and why lionesses hunt in a group. Prepare for a safari!

ELEPHANT

Elephants are found in parts of Africa and the jungles of Asia. Most African elephants live in the savannah, where it is hot and there is very little rain each year. They wander across huge areas of land looking for water and food.

FOOTPRINT
An elephant has large, round, flat feet to carry its broad, heavy body.

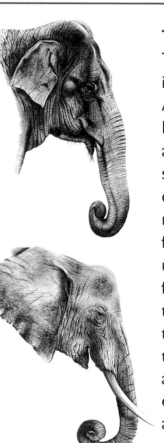

TWO TYPES
The Asian elephant is smaller than the African elephant. Its ears are smaller and its tusks are shorter. Asian elephants do not roam beyond the forests where they usually live because food is plentiful there. They are easy to tame and are trained to carry logs and people. African elephants, however, are difficult to train.

WATER ROUTES
In the hot savannah weather, the rivers often dry out. Elephants travel long distances in search of water. The oldest female leads the way. She knows hidden paths through the bush because her mother taught them to her. She teaches the other elephants so that the herd will always find rare water holes.

DRINKING HABITS

To drink, an elephant sucks water up its trunk and then squeezes the tip shut. It puts the trunk into its mouth and gushes the water down its throat.

COOLING DOWN

Elephants do not sweat. To keep cool, they wallow in water or roll in the mud. The mud works as a sun block and keeps them cool. It also protects them from insect bites.

Elephants spend a lot of time looking for food and water. They sleep only five hours a day. Elephants are herbivores, which means they do not eat meat. They eat grass, leaves, fruit, and bark. An elephant can eat 600 pounds (272 kilograms) of food in one day. When food is scarce in the dry season, elephants may eat soil and small rocks. These add vital salts and minerals to their diet.

UNDER THE BARK
Elephants topple trees so they can eat the flowers and fruit. Their tusks help strip tree bark so the elephants can reach the juicy inner trunk. They leave a path of ruined trees and shrubs behind them.

DIGGING WEAPONS

The African elephant has long, powerful tusks. Each tusk can weigh over 100 pounds (45 kilograms). Sometimes an elephant uses its tusks for digging dry river beds to find underground water. Tusks also help tear and break down the branches of trees. When an elephant is angry or in danger, the tusks are used to fight off attackers.

MOTHERS AND CHILDREN

Elephants live in groups of females and their young. The oldest is called the matriarch. She is the leader. She knows where to find food and water and teaches the others. Teenage males leave the group and live alone all their lives. They seek out female elephants only when they are ready to breed.

9

ZEBRA

Zebras are part of a group of
animals called ungulates. They
have hoofs on their feet and eat
grass. Grazers need to chew their
food well because they cannot
digest hard bits of food. Zebras
live in eastern and southern
Africa. They are often seen with
gnus, giraffes, and springboks.

DUSTY PRINTS
Zebras' hoofs leave
a clear mark in the
dust of the savannah.

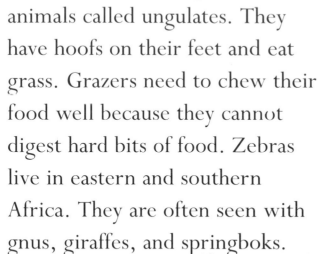

STRIPE SIGNS

There are three kinds of zebra. The plains and the mountain zebra have similar broad, black stripes. Grevy's zebra has a coat of thin stripes. It is also the biggest kind. The mountain zebra is well suited to mountain life because it is small and nimble. The plains and the Grevy's zebra live on the savannah, but never move far from water.

A BIG KICK

A male zebra is called a stallion. He fights by baring his teeth and snorting at the hyena. Kicks from a zebra can kill a hyena.

SAFE CIRCLES

Usually zebras live in harems, which are groups of females and their young protected by a stallion. They sleep at night and graze on short, tough grass during the day. If a lion threatens them, they form a circle around their young. Then they all run to safety.

MEERKAT

Meerkats live in the dry desert of southern Africa. They can go many days without water. They suck moisture from melons and the roots of plants. In hot weather, they dig deep, cool burrows. In winter, they move to shallow parts of the burrow, closer to the sun-warmed earth.

GOOD TOOLS

The front paws are strong hands with long claws. They are used to tear and dig, and for grooming.

A STING IN THE TAIL

Meerkats are good hunters. This scorpion has raised the deadly stinger on its tail.

A QUICK BLOW

With its front paw, the meerkat quickly spins the scorpion over.

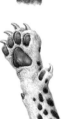

SCENT MARKS

Males leave a scent to mark the area around the entrances to their burrow.

A TASTY MEAL

A sharp bite snaps the poisonous tail, making the scorpion safe to eat.

HUNTING PACK
Meerkats go hunting in groups. They eat insects, ants, beetles, and geckos. They bite or shake their prey to kill it.

HAPPY FAMILIES
Large groups live in burrows made of long tunnels and chambers. Males and females guard the young while the mothers hunt.

SHARING TROUBLE
Meerkats protect each other. Together they chase away intruders such as this bat-eared fox.

RHINOCEROS

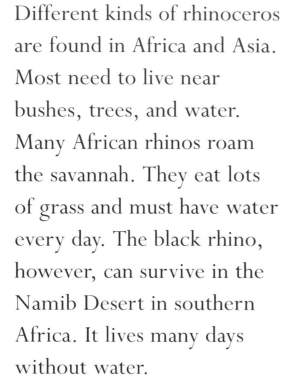

Different kinds of rhinoceros are found in Africa and Asia. Most need to live near bushes, trees, and water. Many African rhinos roam the savannah. They eat lots of grass and must have water every day. The black rhino, however, can survive in the Namib Desert in southern Africa. It lives many days without water.

ALTERNATIVE DIET

The black rhino eats not only grass but roots and shrubs too. This diet helps it to go without water for five days.

CAREFUL BALANCE

The rhinoceros is an ungulate with three hoofs on each foot.

NEIGHBORHOOD SIGNS

Black rhinos do not live together, but share an area. They leave scent trails as a friendly sign to other rhinos. Males will also grunt and bellow to show their presence. Females moo softly.

14

OCCASIONAL MEETINGS

Black rhinos meet only during mating time. Bulls wipe their horns on the ground as they quarrel over a female. The males do not come to blows. When the mating ritual is over, they all return to their own territory.

A LONG CHILDHOOD

A black rhino calf follows its mother. The females form strong bonds with their young, who stay with their mother for up to four years.

SPRINGBOK

On the African grasslands, springboks are hunted by lions, cheetahs, and jackals. Springboks do not have sharp teeth and do not use their horns to defend themselves. Instead, they are alert to every movement and sound, and can run very fast.

HEART SHAPES
Springboks are ungulates. They have a split hoof on each foot.

PRONKING
When attacked by a predator, or hunter, such as a cheetah, springboks make high leaps. Each animal jumps in a different direction. This action is called "pronking."

SAFETY IN NUMBERS
Springboks live among gnus, giraffes, and zebra. These animals warn each other of danger.

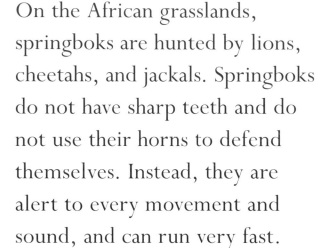

A LOT OF CHEWING

Springboks are herbivores, or plant eaters. They belong to a group of animals, called ruminants, that chew their food twice. After it is chewed and swallowed, the food, or cud, is returned to the mouth for a second chewing. Springboks eat grass, flowers, buds, and fruit. They can go for days without drinking any water.

SAVANNAH WANDERERS

Springboks move in herds and search constantly for food. During the breeding season, the herd breaks into family groups of one male, or buck, and a few females, or does, with their young. The buck frightens away other males by shaking his horns. He marks his family area with a trail of scent and urine.

A SECRET NURSERY

When a doe is about to give birth, she finds a quiet spot. She gives birth to one fawn. This baby spends the first weeks of its life lying hidden in the grass. When it is strong enough to run from predators, it is allowed to join the herd.

GIRAFFE

Giraffes are the tallest animals in the world. They are up to 18 feet (5.5 meters) tall. They are not easy to see, however, if they are standing among trees. This is because their skin pattern blends in with the color of the surroundings. This sort of pattern is called camouflage.

UNBENDING

Giraffes do not need a lot of deep sleep. When they lie down it is only for a few minutes. They find it awkward to bend their neck, so they usually doze standing up. To drink, they bend their knees and stretch their neck to the water. They do not have to drink every day.

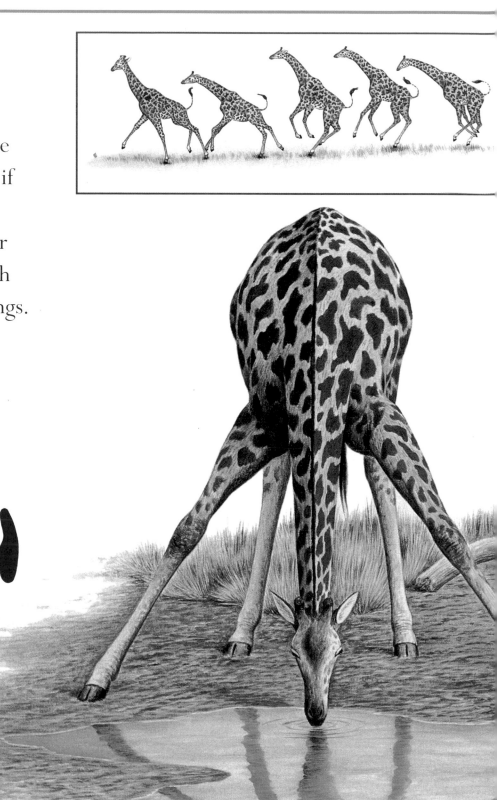

FUNNY WALK
A giraffe has an unusual walk. The front and back legs on each side of the body move together, so the animal rocks from side to side. Giraffes, however, can run as fast as 37 miles (60 kilometers) per hour.

A THORNY DIET
Giraffes live in the drier parts of the savannah in central and southern Africa, where thorny acacia trees grow. Giraffes have very tough lips and a long rubbery tongue so they can eat prickly acacia buds, twigs, and leaves. Giraffes live in herds with up to fifteen members. If one spots a predator, it warns the others with a bark or a coughing noise.

LION

Most wildcats prefer to live alone, but lions like to live in groups. They also hunt together because this makes it easier for them to attack large animals such as water buffalo and zebra. Lions are carnivores, or meat eaters.

A PRIDE

Lions form families of some males and many females with their young. This group is called a "pride of lions."

STRONG ARM TACTICS

The lion has strong muscles in its front legs. It can knock down its prey with one blow of its paw. Lions' claws are long and sharp and easily tear the flesh of a victim.

LION TALK

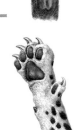

SMELLING
A male lion wrinkles his nose and snarls. He has smelled the urine of a rival.

SNARLING
This lioness is snarling because she is angry.

ROARING
Male lions give loud, deep roars to warn of danger.

HISSING
Lions grunt, meow, or, like this lioness, hiss at each other.

MOTHER SPEAKING
A lioness grunts as her cub jumps on her.

FAMILY DUTIES
The lionesses and their daughters stay in one pride. The lionesses do the hunting. The males protect the young and guard their territory, the area where the lions live and hunt. When young males want to mate, they move to other families.

GALAGO

Galagos are nocturnal, which means they are active at night and sleep during the day. They live in the bushes and trees of the savannah. They can be seen racing around in clumps of prickly acacia trees. They are so nimble they know how to avoid the acacia thorns. Some galagos live in town gardens in South Africa.

LEAPS AND BOUNDS
Galagos race along branches, jumping from tree to tree. They can leap as far as 18 feet (5.5 meters) between trees. They use their tail to help them land. On the ground, they hop like kangaroos or scuttle along on all fours with their tail stuck in the air.

GOOD CATCH
Galagos eat moths, grasshoppers, and many kinds of beetles. They catch their prey by pouncing and grabbing. Sometimes they creep up on the insects or even snatch them out of the air.

LITTLE HANDS
Galagos have hands with nails on each finger. Their thumb helps them pick up and hold things.

BABY CARE

Galagos build leafy nests or settle in tree hollows. After giving birth, a mother keeps her babies in the nest for a few days. Then she takes them along when she hunts. She carries them on her back.

BUSH BABIES

In South Africa, galagos are called "bush babies" because they are small. Some are only the size of a person's hand. They also have this name because their wailing sounds like babies crying.

HIPPOPOTAMUS

A hippopotamus is the size of a small car. Its skin looks tough, but it is sensitive to heat. To avoid the strong rays of the African sun, the hippo wallows in mud and water all day. To breathe, it pokes its nostrils above the surface. At night, it eats plants on the water's edge or goes inland for grass and fruit.

BAD TEMPERS
Male hippos often fight to control their territory or win females. They roar and snap. Some injure or even kill one another!

MUDDY FEET
Hippos' toes are slightly webbed. Their feet are suited to mud and water. Hippos do not walk long distances but they can move very fast when they are chasing an enemy.

WATER BIRTH

Sometimes a hippo mother gives birth in water. She quickly lifts her new born to the surface so that it can breathe.

CHANGING PATTERNS

Hippos live in large groups but these move and change. Mothers look after their young for many years. Females gather with their young of all ages. Males may form their own groups. Sometimes males, females, and their young all gather together. They follow well-known paths and eat at familiar grass patches, which are called "hippo lawns."

LEOPARD

Leopards live in parts of Africa and of Asia. They live and hunt in a territory called their "home range." They mark it by spraying urine on trees. They are very shy and spend their lives hunting, eating, and sleeping alone. When they are two years old, cubs leave their mother and find their own territory.

CLAWS AND PADS

A leopard uses its sharp claws to climb trees and attack prey. The padded paws help the leopard land softly when it leaps from trees and rocks.

A SHARP TONGUE

The leopard's tongue is covered with tiny, sharp hairs. Before the leopard eats its prey, it licks the body. The tongue strips patches of fur off the dead animal.

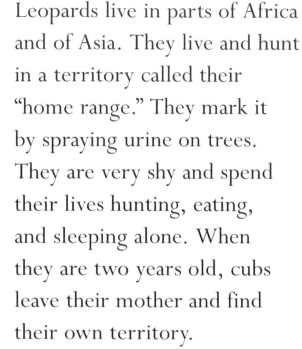

CAT CALLS

Leopards make a throaty barking sound when they are looking for a mate. Babies, or cubs, make a humming noise when feeding from their mother.

CUNNING HUNTER

The leopard is a fast and clever hunter. Sometimes it snakes through the grass on its belly, then charges and springs onto its prey. The Asian cloud leopard hangs from a branch, then leaps from the tree onto the other animal. Its claws and teeth tear at the victim.

Leopards do not like the heat, so they rest on the leafy branches of trees or under high rocks. They are well hidden because their spotted coats blend into leaves and shadows. These high places are "look-out" posts where a leopard can watch for attackers and prey. Female leopards give birth in caves or thick bushes.

EARLY LESSONS
Cubs are kept hidden until they are about six weeks old. They are very playful, but are taught to hunt at an early age. The mother prepares them for life on their own.

LEOPARD PREY
Leopards are nocturnal. They rest during the day and hunt at night or in the early dawn. There is a wide choice of prey on the savannah. If they live near people and farms, leopards will hunt sheep or pet dogs. People rarely can catch the swift, silent killer. Leopards fear only lions, who will fight or kill them to steal their prey.

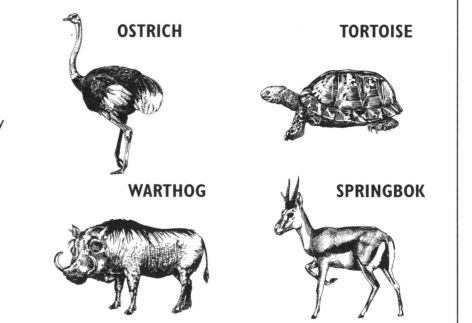

OSTRICH

TORTOISE

WARTHOG

SPRINGBOK

BEYOND REACH

Leopards do not gulp down their prey in one sitting. They eat it over several days. This means they must guard the meal from scavengers. These are animals that do not hunt for their own food, but instead eat what other animals have killed. This leopard has dragged a carcass, or dead body, up a tree for safe keeping. A hyena slinks round the trunk. It is hungry and can smell the meat.

CROCODILE

Crocodiles change their
body heat with the weather.
They bask in the sun to
warm up. When their body
temperature becomes too
hot, they slip into the river.
In the hot savannah, they
spend hours in the water
or lying very still in the shade.

WARMING EGGS
Eggs are laid in mounds of earth and
rotting plants. The female keeps the
eggs warm with her body.

DOUBLE WALK
Crocodiles hold their
legs straight to walk.
In the water, their
strong back legs and
webbed back feet help
them swim swiftly.

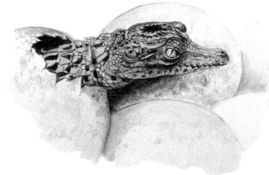

FIRST SOUNDS
As they hatch,
babies grunt.
The mother then
knows they are born.

CROCODILE CARE
The mother takes her young to the river after they hatch.
She cares for them for several weeks.

A DAMP LIFE

Crocodiles are semi-aquatic. They must live in or near water but cannot live underwater.

SCARY SNAPPER

Their long snouts and sharp teeth snap and kill fish or animals drinking at the river. They snap at humans too, so people in Africa are very careful near rivers.

HEAD START

A crocodile's eyes and nostrils are set high on its head so the animal can see and breathe while floating in the water. It has no lips. Its teeth clutch at the prey. The food is not chewed, but instead swallowed in chunks.

INDEX

C
Crocodile 30, 31

G
Galago 22, 23

H
Hippopotamus 24, 25
Hyena 11, 29

L
Leopard 26, 27,
        28, 29
Lion 20, 21

M
Meerkat 12, 13

R
Rhinoceros 14, 15,

S
Scorpion 12
Springbok 10, 16, 17

T
Tortoise 28

U
Ungulate 10, 14

Z
Zebra 10, 11, 16, 20

GLOSSARY

Carnivore - An animal that eats mainly meat

Camouflage - Many animals have a coat or skin that blends with the color of the place where they live. This is called camouflage. Camouflage hides an animal from predators, or prey it is trying to catch.

Harem - A group of female animals, their young, and an adult male

Herbivore - An animal that feeds mainly on plants

Mammal - An animal that does not lay eggs but gives birth to its young. A mammal mother produces milk to feed her baby.

Migrate - Animals migrate when they travel long distances to find food, warmth or to breed.

Nocturnal - An animal that is active at night

Predator - An animal that hunts other animals

Prey - An animal that is hunted by another animal

Ruminant - An animal that chews its food twice over before digesting it

Scavenger - An animal that eats what other animals have killed

Territory - The area marked out by an animal as its living space

Ungulate - An animal that has hoofs

1 2 3 4 5 6 7 8 9 0   Printed in the U.S.A. 7 6 5 4 3 2 1 0 9 8